By Every Word

By
Chuck Wyeth
L.B. Bramble

Charleston, AR:
COBB PUBLISHING
2022

Published in the United States of America by:

Cobb Publishing
CobbPublishing.com
Editor@CobbPublishing.com
479-747-8372

Unless otherwise noted, all Scripture references come from the New King James Version, copyright Thomas Nelson. Used with permission.

ISBN: 978-1-960858-31-3

Contents

Introduction

Without the Bible, mankind is completely lost, hopeless, without any knowledge of salvation. And even if one could know somehow that salvation was possible, without the Bible, you have no idea how to find it!

Thank God (literally) He gave us His word. In it, He introduces Himself to each of us. In it, He displays His love and grace for sinners (like Abraham, David, and Saul of Tarsus), while also displaying His wrath toward the unrepentant (like Korah, Balaam, and Jezebel).

Since the Bible is the only original source for knowledge about the life and teachings of Jesus, it is to there we must go if we want to know about Him—the one whose blood takes away our sin.

Without using the Bible, it is *impossible* to know the answer to the question, "What must I do to be saved?"

But since the Bible was written, men with pet theories and unbiblical doctrines (and often desires to be famous) have led astray millions—all the while claiming the Bible backs up their anti-Christian teachings.

Why have these false teachings persisted? It is for one reason: *People are not reading and studying the word of God.*

This short volume is designed to point you to the word of God. To show how essential it is to your life. To encourage you to read for yourself what God says, instead of relying on "My pastor said…"

If reading the Bible has ever seemed intimidating to you, this book will give you the encouragement and motivation to dive right in.

Bradley S. Cobb
Author, *The Holy Spirit in the Book of Acts* and *War in Heaven, War on Earth: what Revelation meant to the original readers and what it means for us today*

We wrote this book to answer some very important questions about God's word. First, How important is it to our lives? Second, How do I apply it to my everyday life? And finally, How do I find what the truth is among all the different messages coming from the religious world?

We hope that this writing is a blessing to all who read it.

The Authors

Then Jesus was led up by the Spirit into the wilderness to be tempted by the devil. And when He had fasted 40 days and 40 nights, afterward He was hungry. Now when the tempter came to Him, He said, "If you are the son of God, command that these stones become bread." But He answered and said, "It is written, 'Man shall not live by bread alone, but by every word that proceeds from the mouth of God.'"
(Matthew 4:1-4)

"Word" in Greek is "rhema," [hray'-mah]; an utterance; by implication, a "matter" or "topic." The significance of rhema (as distinct from logos) is exemplified in the injunction to take "the sword of the Spirit, which is the word of God." Ephesians 6:17

By Every Word

Section 1:

What Is the Word of God?

First, let me explain what the Bible is. "Bible" comes from the Greek word "biblos," which means a book, or a collection of writings. In ancient times, these writings were contained in scrolls. The Bible as we know it today is the most widely read book in the world, and was written over a span of some 1,500 years with approximately 35 writers.

All these writers had a close relationship with God. This is important! Most writers in the Old Testament were prophets of God. Their writings were meticulously copied through the years by scribes, men who copied each scroll exactly as it was originally written. Even the slightest mistake meant you had to burn the whole scroll-in-progress, and start all over again. New Testament writings were originally written by apostles or those closely related to them. These books and letters were read, referenced, and studied extensively by the early church. The accuracy of our copies of these writings has been confirmed through the many handwritten copies and fragments (literally thousands) that have been found. Together, these writings present the history of man, his sin against God, and God's solution: sending His only begotten Son so people's sins might be forgiven.

> *All Scripture is given by **inspiration** of God, and is profitable for doctrine, for reproof, for correction, for instruction in righteousness, that the man of God may be complete, thoroughly equipped for every good work. (2 Timothy 3:16)*

The word "**inspiration**" comes from the Greek word, theopneustos [theh-op'-nyoo-stos]; which has a basic meaning of "divinely breathed in," "given by inspiration of God."

Therefore, through these writings, God presented what He wanted the world to know. Even Jesus said in John 14:24, *"He who does not love Me does not keep My words; and **the***

word which you hear is not mine *but the **Father's*** *who sent me."* Jesus was instructed by God on what to say and do while He was here. The words he brought were not His own; they were from His Father (i.e., God).

The text itself, from beginning to end, Old Testament and New Testament, blend together as if one person was behind it all. That one person is "God."

2 Timothy 3:16 goes on to explain what the word of God is profitable for:

1. **<u>Doctrine</u>** this comes from the Greek word didaskalia [did-as-kal-ee'-ah], which denotes instruction: "that which is taught, doctrine." That is, doctrine means "a teaching." It is what you learn. We all need a basic understanding of God's will, and this only comes from God's complete word.

2. **<u>Reproof</u>** comes from the Greek word elegchos [el'-eng-khos]; which means "proof, conviction: – evidence, reproof." **Reproof** means to rebuke, which expresses sharp disapproval or

criticism of someone due to their misbehavior or inappropriate actions. Therefore, the Scriptures can be used to show a brother or sister their behavior or actions are not in line with God, and that their soul may be in jeopardy.

3. **Correction** comes from the Greek word epanorthosis [ep-an-or'-tho-sis]; a straightening up again, rectification (reformation): correction. "A restoration to an upright or right state." Tying *correction* to the previous word *reproof*, the Scriptures are a guide for Christians to correct their behavior and walk uprightly before God. In other words, repenting of incorrect actions, replacing them with correct actions please God.

4. **Instruction** comes from the Greek word paideia [pahee-di'-ah]; tutorage, (education or training,) as in "the training of a child, including instruction"; hence, "discipline, correction," "chastening (nurture)," a discipline that regulates character. The word of God therefore is an instruction book that leads, through proper study, to the

knowledge, wisdom and understanding God desires us to have. We change from a corrupted person, to a person who walks in uprightness, with decency, virtue, and good morals. When we accept the gospel, we begin as children who have only received basic instruction, sometimes referred to as the milk of the word. As time goes on and we become more knowledgeable, we graduate from milk to meat, sometimes called the meat of the word. This includes a more in-depth study of what sin is, so we can avoid it (1 John 2:1). We also learn how to properly handle all situations we run into during our lifetime.

When you put these words together, you should see how a Christian is "thoroughly equipped for every good work" by using only God's inspired word. Upon becoming a Christian, one is like a child who needs to be nurtured and taught the Scriptures (i.e., *doctrine*), to cultivate a righteous character. Occasionally one may need *correction* or a restoration to an upright state to be pleasing to

God. The Bible, God's instructions to us, contains everything needed to be taught by the teacher and studied by the student to live correctly before God.

Now, to the phrase, *"complete, thoroughly equipped for every good work."* Think about this, you spend most of your time away from the congregation of God's people. Therefore, you do most of your work/living away from the church, while you are on your own. Everything you do in life, regardless of where you are, can be guided by the light of God's word.

Look at how biblical writers viewed the word of God. Jesus, praying for the disciples, said, *"Sanctify them by Your truth. <u>Your word is truth</u>"* (John 17:17). Jesus asked God to sanctify (i.e., bless, approve, and purify) them. Therefore, you are approved and purified by obedience to God's word.

Paul said *"Paul, a bondservant of God and an apostle of Jesus Christ, according to the faith of God's elect and the acknowledg-*

ment *of the truth* which *accords* (i.e., is in harmony) *with godliness, in hope of eternal life which God, who cannot lie, promised before time began, but has in due time manifested His word through preaching, which was committed to me according to the commandment of God our Savior"* (Titus 1:1-3). The obvious conclusion of these two passages is, <u>God cannot lie</u>! So, what He promises, will be done! We can trust God to be true to His word! And that promise was made "*even before* ***time*** *began*." (The King James Version states "*before the* ***world*** *began*.") The Greek word used here is aionios [ahee-o'-nee-os]; this word has been translated as "perpetual," "eternal," "everlasting," "the world began," "since the world began" and "forever."

According to Romans 16:12; 2 Timothy 1:9; and Titus 1:2; "*it is according to the revelation of the mystery, which* <u>*was secret since the world began.*</u>" This now-revealed secret is for our assurance and, because God cannot lie, the promises made to us will be kept. We can have full confidence and trust in God's word to be true. It is all we need as Christians to teach, study, live by, and please God. But the emphasis must be on the entirety of God's word, as Jesus said, *"by every word that proceeds out of the mouth of God."* (Matthew 4:4)

One of the things a Christian should have is *"the sword of the Spirit, which is the **word** of God"* (Ephesians 6:17). "Word" here is translated from the same word as Matthew 4:4, "by every **word**." It is a requirement for every person who follows God through Jesus Christ our Lord. This sword of the spirit is also immensely powerful. Look At Hebrews 4:12; *"For the **word** of God is living and powerful, and sharper than any two-edged sword, piercing even to the division of soul and spirit, and of the joints and the marrow, and is a discerner of the thoughts and intents of the heart."* [1]

Think about that for a minute. Have you ever wondered why people find God's word so hard to hear? Many become evasive and

---

[1] **Note:** Here, the "**word**" comes from the Greek word logos, log'-os; something said (including the thought); by implication, a topic (subjects of discourse), also reasoning (the mental faculty or motive).

defensive when it is spoken. Do you think that might be a sign their actions are not in accordance with God's will? Remember Romans 3:23; *"For all have sinned and fall short of the glory of God."*

We have all made mistakes. To God, these are sins, which have separated us from Him. God's word is a guide to show us what we did wrong, and how to get back to Him. His word, the Bible, shows us we must stop sinful behavior; but it also shows we need God's forgiveness for sinful things we've already done. Without the Bible, we would be completely without hope in knowing how to obtain this forgiveness.

According to Romans 3:24, we can be, "justified freely by His grace through the redemption that is in Christ Jesus: whom God hath set forth to be a propitiation through faith in His blood, to declare His righteousness for the remission of sins that are past, through the forbearance of God." (KJV) Clearly, God can and will forgive us for our sins if we obey the word He has given us. It tells us how to get back to Him and have eternal life with Him through His only begotten son, Jesus Christ.

> *And every priest stands ministering daily and offering repeatedly the same sacrifices, which can never take away sins. But this Man, (i.e., Jesus) after He had offered one sacrifice for sins forever, sat down at the right hand of God, from that time waiting till His enemies are made His footstool. For by one offering He has perfected forever those who are being sanctified (Hebrews 10:11-14, KJV).*

Just a little background here: under the Old Testament, the children of Israel needed to sacrifice perfect animals yearly for their sins. The fact they had to do it over and over shows it was not a perfect sacrifice for sin. Therefore Jesus, "who was without sin" (2 Corinthians 5:21 & 1 John 3:5), and referred to as "the Lamb of God" (John 1:29, Revelation 12:11, 17:14), had to come and die upon the cross, a perfect sacrifice for sin that was once for all time.

Think about it this way, God's word tells us that, once we have obeyed the gospel, we are set free from sin like prisoners pardoned from jail. And once free, we strive to avoid sin, which tries to put us back in the same prison!

Many people fail to remember two simple facts. First, *"Man shall not live by bread alone, but by every word that proceeds from the mouth of God"* (Matthew 4:4). Second, Jesus said, *"if anyone hears My words and does not believe, I do not judge him; for I did not come to judge the world but to save the world. He who rejects Me, and does not receive My words, has that which judges him— the word that I have spoken will judge him in the last day"* (John 12:47-48). Remember what Jesus said in John 14:24, *"He who does not love Me does not keep My words; and the word which you hear is not mine but the Fathers who sent me."* The words which judge us are God's!

Putting these verses together, you can see, not only are we to live by every word that proceeds out of the mouth of God, but we will be judged by those same God-breathed words—the Scripture!

For those who disobey, Hebrews 10:31 states, "It is a fearful thing to fall into the hands of the living God" (KJV). Also, Romans 6:23; "For the wages of sin is death; but the gift of God is eternal life through Jesus Christ our Lord" (KJV).

On the other hand, for those who obey, Jesus says in John 14:23-24, "If anyone loves Me, he will keep My word; and My Father will love him, and We will come to him and make Our home with him. He who does not love Me does not keep my words; and the word which you hear is not mine but the Father's who sent me." On Judgment Day, do we really want to be found not living in compliance with God's complete word?

Section 2:

How do we approach God's word?

This is a most important question. If we do not have the correct attitude when we study the word of God, how can we ever hope to come to a clear and decisive understanding?

> *But the hour is coming, and now is, when the true worshipers will worship the Father in spirit and truth; for the Father is seeking such to worship Him. God is spirit, and those who worship Him must worship in spirit and truth (John 4:23-24).*

God is not flesh like we are, God is spirit. When we read or study God's word, we should do it in the same manner as worshiping Him. This is further tied to "truth," which can only be attained through study of all the relevant facts.

> *Then Jesus said to those Jews who believed Him, "If you abide in My word, you are My disciples indeed. And you*

shall know the truth, and the truth shall make you free" (John 8:31-32).

In a world where so many beliefs contradict one another (not to mention contradicting the Bible), it makes it even more imperative that we approach God's word with and open mind and a "God, teach me what I need to know" attitude. 2 Timothy 2:15 puts it this way; *"Be diligent to present yourself approved to God, a worker who does not need to be ashamed, accurately handling the word of truth"* (NASB). This emphasizes the importance of listening closely to what God is telling us. We must be hard-working and meticulous in our study of God's word to make sure understand it properly.

Consider for instance, when you are taking a class in school. You cannot go in with a preconceived idea of how the subject should be approached. You must approach it with an open mind, looking closely at what is presented about that subject. Yet many approach God's word with preconceived ideas heard from other people, without ever studying to see if those things are true.

Let's face it, in our lives we talk to people with many different attitudes about every subject under the sun. But when it comes to God's word, <u>the only thing that matters is what God says</u>. If we have no one around us that knows the truth (in other words, has never really studied God's word and does not know the facts), we can end up with some bizarre concepts. The "I heard it from someone else who did not check the facts," or "just a personal belief due to conversations with friends, family, or peer pressure" arguments will not be a sound defense on Judgment Day. Just look at the world, and the many contradicting beliefs. They cannot *all* be correct when compared to God's word.

> *Beloved, do not believe every spirit, but test the spirits, whether they are of God; because many false prophets have gone out into the world (1 John 4:1).*

You would do well to read 1, 2, 3 John as well as the book of Jude for yourselves, and see how the apostles combatted false teachers and antichrists even in their day.

Think about that for a second: when you go to the source, all those preconceived comments, notions, and thoughts must be put away to see the truth. You must start with a clean slate and open mind. The study of God's word is most important—your very spiritual life hangs in the balance! It's imperative to understand God's will for us. And, as with any subject, the more you study and have a clear base of understanding to build on, the easier it is to comprehend and separate false concepts from the truth God desires us to know.

> *And even if our gospel is veiled, it is veiled to those who are perishing. In their case the god of this world has blinded the minds of the unbelievers, to keep them from seeing the light of the gospel of the glory of Christ, who is the image of God. (2 Corinthians 4:3-4, ESV)[2]*

---

[2] If you desire a greater understanding of this, review the explanation Jesus gave in the Parable of the Sower in Matthew 13:16-23.

Remember what we saw earlier: we are to live by every word that proceeds out of the mouth of God, and that we will be judged by those same words. Remember also what Jesus said in John 8:31-32, *"If you continue in my word, then you are truly my disciples; and you will know the truth, and the truth will set you free"* (NASB). Notice, it is *the truth of God's word* that truly *sets us free*, not the false concepts of man.

When I teach, I never expect anyone to believe what I say just because I say it. Likewise, I never expect anyone to disbelieve what I say just because I say it. Think about this Scripture again, *"Be diligent to present yourself approved to God as a worker who does not need to be ashamed, accurately handling the word of truth"* (2 Timothy 2:15, NASB). Each of us has a command from God to not only try every spirit, but to study to show ourselves approved unto God. We are also supposed to rightly handle the word of truth. That means we must study it with an open mind, with determination, to achieve the correct understanding. If God did not know we were capable of doing this, he would not be expecting us to do it. But God knows every one of us has that capability, because God himself gave it to us.

Section 3:

Love—the Two Greatest Commandments

Jesus was asked what the greatest commandment was. His response is found in Matthew 22:37-40:

> *You shall love the Lord your God with all your heart, and with all your soul, and with all your mind. This is the greatest and foremost commandment. The second is like it, you shall love your neighbor as yourself. On these two commandments depend the whole Law and the Prophets.*

Moses, who with God's help, brought the children of Israel out of Egypt, states in Deuteronomy 6:4-5, "*Hear, O Israel: The Lord our God, the Lord is one. Love the Lord your God with all your heart and with all your soul and with all your strength*" (NIV). The word of God is totally based on the concept of love of God and the love of the people around us, our neighbors. And think of what it says in John 3:16: "For God so loved the world that

He gave His only begotten Son, that whoever believes in Him should not perish but have everlasting life."

From the very beginning, God desired mankind show Him the same love that He has shown for us. But man keeps sinning and going in the other direction. So God, out of love for each and every one of us, sent His only begotten Son to suffer and die on the cross and pay for our sins. Out of love, He gave us a chance to make things right with Him and spend eternity in heaven. That is a very faithful love!

But notice the second part Jesus mentioned: loving our neighbors as we love ourselves. Much of what we have in the Bible concerns how we interact with and treat one another. Notice the following verse:

> *If someone says, "I love God," and hates his brother, he is a liar; for the one who does not love his brother whom he has seen, cannot love God whom he has not seen (1 John 4:20, NASB).*

So, how we love one another is going to be part of the basis of our final judgment before God. Read the judgment scene at the end of Matthew 25 for even more confirmation of this. We can look at this in the opposite way as well, because our love must be properly directed. Read what John wrote:

> *Do not love the world, or anything in the world. If anyone loves the world, love of the Father is not in them. For everyone in the world, the lust of the flesh, the lust of the eyes and the pride of life, comes not from the Father, but is from the world. The world and its desires pass away, but whoever does the will of God lives forever (1 John 2:15-17, NIV).*

Many today hold the things of this world in remarkably high esteem; so much so, they feel they have no need for God. They have forgotten all these things will be destroyed in the end. And look at how people treat one another, lying, stealing, pushing drugs, coveting their neighbor's goods, and looking for ways they can profit off everyone else. Where is the love in all that?

> *But the day of the Lord will come as a thief in the night, in which the heavens will pass away with a great noise, and the elements will melt with fervent heat; both the earth and the works that are in it will be burned up. Therefore, since all these things will be dissolved, what manner of persons ought you to be in holy conduct and godliness, looking for and hastening the coming of the day of God, because of which the heavens will be dissolved, being on fire, and the elements will melt with fervent heat? (2 Peter 3:10-12)*

All the works of man will come to an end with destruction, and we are told what happens to those whose affection is on worldly things:

> *You adulterous people! Do you not know that friendship with the world is enmity with God? Therefore, whoever wishes to be a friend of the world*

makes himself an enemy of God (James 4:4, ESV).

Take a look at the next three verses.

I have given them your word, and the world has hated them because <u>they are not of the world</u>, just as I am not of the world. I do not ask that you take them out of the world, but that you keep them from the evil one. They are not of the world, just as I am not of the world (John 17:14-16, ESV).

If you were of the world, the world would love you as its own; but because <u>you are not of the world</u>, but I chose you out of the world, therefore the world hates you (John 15:19, ESV).

They [those who do not confess Christ came in the flesh] are from the world; therefore they speak from the world, and the world listens to them (1 John 4:5, ESV, see also verse 3).

Christians are, in the spiritual sense, not of this world. In contrast, those of the world only listen to those in the world, being separate from Christ and His followers. The reason for this is as follows:

"For as many of you as were baptized into Christ have put on Christ" (Galatians 3:27). Also look at the great commission given to the disciples in Matthew 28:18-20:

> *And Jesus came to them and spoke unto them, saying, All authority hath been given unto me in heaven and on earth. Go ye therefore, and make disciples of all the nations, baptizing them into the name of the Father and of the Son and of the Holy Spirit: teaching them to observe all things whatsoever I commanded you: and lo, I am with you always, even unto the end of the world (ASV).*

In Acts 2, on the day of Pentecost, Peter spoke and many were added to the church, transferring them from an earthly citizenship to members of the heavenly kingdom through Christ. It would be good to read the whole section but let us just look at a few verses.

Now when they heard this they were cut to the heart, and said to Peter and the rest of the apostles, "Brothers, what shall we do?" And Peter said to them, "Repent and be baptized every one of you in the name of Jesus Christ for the forgiveness of your sins, and you will receive the gift of the Holy Spirit. For the promise is for you and for your children and for all who are far off, everyone whom the Lord our God calls to himself." And with many other words he bore witness and continued to exhort them, saying, "Save yourselves from this crooked generation." So those who received his word were baptized, and there were added that day about three thousand souls." (Acts 2:37-41, ESV)

Galatians 3:27 shows those who were baptized, were baptized into Christ, and have put on Christ. Put that with Acts 2:37-41: they were baptized for the remission of sins. They also were told they would receive a baptismal portion of the Holy Spirit, which I be-

lieve refers to putting on Christ (like in Galatians 3:27). The main point is true Christians
are no longer citizens of this world and do not
look at themselves as such. They know their
membership is in a heavenly kingdom. Just
because we are still living in this world, does
not mean we should partake of old lusts and
pleasures that we once indulged in. When we
repent, we turned our back on those things
didn't we? In 1 Peter 2:11, Christians are referred to as <u>sojourners</u> and <u>pilgrims</u>, reflect-
ing our true citizenship in the kingdom of
heaven as we sojourn here in this earthly
realm, just like people here visiting other
countries where they are not citizens.

As this section talks about friendship with
the world being *enmity* with God, let me tell
you a story.

I grew up on a farm, I understand where
food comes from, because we raised it. We
also raised cows for milk, so I know where
milk comes from as well. Imagine my sur-
prise when a person from the city declared on
a news broadcast, "I don't care what happens
to farms! I get all my food from the grocery

store!" This person had no concept that food in the grocery store came from farms. I say this because when you look around at all the things here, you need to realize the world isn't where they came from—this world is like the grocery store. All these things came from God! The very first verse of the Bible says, *"In the beginning God created the heavens and the earth"* (KJV). All the elements, animals, plants, everything in this entire universe is created by God. We use these things to create various tools for ourselves, such as cars, houses, computers etc. But they all come from God.

People care so much about this world, care about the things molded out of God's creation, but ignore our all-powerful God and Creator. It does not matter if it's a cell phone, computer, car, diamond ring, or money; all the elements used by man were first created by God for our use. Why wouldn't God get upset with us for caring more about these created objects than our Creator Himself? I can clearly understand why caring for the things of this world above God is considered **enmity** (*i.e., hostility, hatred, animosity*) against

Him. Does that help you see how important this will be on the day of judgment? Caring for the things of this world cannot be considered love toward God. Remember, a true Christian is like a traveler in a foreign country, they may have to obey the laws of that country, but they owe their allegiance and loyalty to the country where they have their citizenship.

A question then arises, who is the god of this world? Who are people really following before being baptized into Christ for the remission of sins? Consider –

> *You are of your father the devil, and your will is to do your father's desires. He was a murderer from the beginning, and does not stand in the truth, because there is no truth in him. When he lies, he speaks out of his own character, for he is a liar and the father of lies (John 8:44, ESV).*

> *And you were dead in the trespasses and sins in which you once walked, following the course of this world, following the prince of the power of the air*

[another name for the devil /Satan], *the spirit that is now at work in the sons of disobedience— among whom we all once lived in the passions of our flesh, carrying out the desires of the body and the mind, and were by nature children of wrath, like the rest of mankind (Ephesians 2:1-3, ESV).*

In their case the god of this world has blinded the minds of the unbelievers, to keep them from seeing the light of the gospel of the glory of Christ, who is the image of God (2 Corinthians 4:4, ESV).

We first see in John 8:44, that "*the devil is a murderer from the beginning.*" And he does not stand for the truth because "*he is a liar.*" In fact, he is "*the father of lies!*"

We then learn in Ephesians 2:1-3, before becoming Christians, we were actually following Satan as we followed the regular course of this world.

We all once lived in the passions of our flesh, carrying out the desires of the body and the mind, and were by nature children of wrath, like the rest of mankind.

Moving on to 2 Corinthians 4:4, we see unbelievers are being blinded by Satan to keep them from seeing the light of the gospel of Christ that can save them.

Friendship with the world is embracing, once again, the passions of our flesh, body, and mind, re-engaging into the thoughts of Satan, allowing his will to again enter us and control us. Friendship of the world is a fleshly mindset that can and will lead us to destruction.

How does all this fit in with our topic, that <u>God loves us and we are to love him in return</u>? Think about Jesus' words in Luke 6:46, *"And why do you call me, Lord, Lord, and do not do what I say?"* and John 14:15, *"If you love Me, keep My commandments."* Keeping God's commandments are the way we prove our love for Him and our love for our Lord and Savior Jesus Christ.

Let us look at this from another direction using these Scriptures.

> *Do you not know that "to whom you present yourselves slaves to obey," you are that one's slaves whom you obey, whether of sin leading to death, or of obedience leading to righteousness? (Romans 6:16)*

> *No one can serve two masters; for either he will hate the one and love the other, or else he will be loyal to the one and despise the other. You cannot serve God and mammon. (Matthew 6:24)*

The point here is, you cannot serve God and the world, i.e., two masters. Rationally, you can see there would be conflict between the love of God and the love of Mammon (i.e., money), a worldly concept of wealth. If money is what controls you, then it is not God. Likewise, if it is God's love controlling you, you will not be controlled by money. You should "*Keep your lives free from the love of money and be content with what you have, because God has said, 'Never will I leave you; never will I forsake you.'"* (Hebrews 13:5, NIV). A Christian clearly has to make a choice.

This works as well for other things. Take the times when someone hurt you by some action. To follow Christ, we look to Scriptures such as Romans 12:18-21:

> *If possible, so far as it depends on you, be at peace with all men. Never take your own revenge, beloved, but leave room for the wrath of God, for it is written, "Vengeance is mine, I will repay," says the Lord. "But if your enemy is hungry, feed him, and if he is thirsty, give him drink; for in so doing you will heap burning coals upon his head. Do not be overcome by evil, but overcome evil with good." (ESV)*

> *Vengeance is mine, and recompense [i.e., payment or compensation for their evil deeds], for the time when their foot shall slip; for the day of their calamity is at hand, and their doom comes swiftly.' (Deuteronomy 32:35, ESV)*

In these verses, the love of God and our love for one another takes precedence over any desire we have for revenge. We are to overcome evil with good. Ultimately, we will all be judged. Those that do evil will not escape God's judgment, so leave it to the Lord.

> *For not even the Father judges anyone, but He has given all judgment to the Son, so that all will honor the Son just as they honor the Father. The one who does not honor the Son does not honor the Father who sent Him. (John 5:22-23, NASB)*

Remember, we are to live by every word that comes out of the mouth of God (Matthew 4:4), and Jesus is the one who brought us His word. Remember also John 14:24, *"He who does not love Me does not keep My words; and the word which you hear is not mine but the Fathers who sent me."* And John 12:47-48:

> *If anyone hears My words and does not believe, I do not judge him; for I did not come to judge the world but to save the world. He who rejects Me, and*

does not receive My words, has that which judges him—the word that I have spoken will judge him in the last day.

The judgment we will all experience will be a comparing of our actions and words to the words Jesus brought to us from the Father (i.e., God.)

Section 4:

The Word of God vs. Change.

Many people believe that as civilization changes, God's word needs to change to keep up. Let's see how this idea compares to Scripture.

- **Malachi 3:6:** "*For I am the Lord, I do not change*." God's own words that he does not change cannot be any clearer.

- **2 Peter 3:8:** "*But, beloved, do not forget this one thing, that with the Lord one day is as a thousand years, and a thousand years as one day.*" God is not like the rest of us (James 4:4). We change our minds constantly about many things. On the other hand, God does not change, over a day or over a thousand years. To God, it could be as thought Christ's death on the cross was just 2 days ago. After planning this all out before the universe was created, why would God change

His mind after (in his eyes) just two days?

- **1 Corinthians 14:33**: *"For God is not the author of confusion, but of peace, as in all churches of the saints"* (NASB). The execution of God's plan, and the literal execution of His only begotten son, is the victory over death and sin. The battle is already won! It would not make sense for Him to change anything at this point! And if God were to change His mind, think how confusing it would be. We can say with confidence that the word of God is constant and He will not alter it.

- **1 Peter 1:24b & Isaiah 40:8**: *"The grass withers, the flower fades, but the word of our God will stand forever."* (ESV)

The Father does not change, but Scripture is also clear that Jesus does not change. Thus, His words still remain in force. He was serious when He said, *"The words I speak will judge you in the last day."*

- **Hebrews 13:8**, *"Jesus Christ is the same yesterday and today and forever"* (NIV).

- **Matthew 24:35** (also found in **Luke 21:33**): *"Heaven and earth will pass away, but My words will by no means pass away."* Think about that for a minute, this implies even to the end of the earth (which could be an exceedingly long time if God so willed), His words will not pass away. I don't know how it can be made any clearer that the word of God does not change—regardless of whether man or culture changes. In other words, if we are to be pleasing to God, we must live according to His words exactly as they are given to us. Loving God and loving others is a command that will not change. **Love does not change!**

- **Hebrews 13:7-9,** *"Remember your leaders, those who spoke to you the word of God. Consider the outcome of their way of life and imitate their* *faith. Jesus Christ is the same yesterday and today and forever. **Do not be led away by diverse and strange teachings**, for it is good for the heart to be strengthened by grace, not by foods, which have not benefited those devoted to them"* (ESV). This is encouragement and a warning put together.

First a little background; the church is overseen scripturally by bishops (also called elders in Titus 1:5-7) and deacons whose qualifications are found in 1 Timothy 3:1-13. The term "bishop" comes from the Greek word episkopos [ep-is'-kop-os]; a superintendent, (i.e., officer in general charge of a [or the] church), overseer. Also called "elders," which comes from the Greek word presbuterros [pres-boo'-ter-os]; an elder, old man, eldest, a senior. They have primary oversight of a local congregation only. And there is *no scriptural authority* for any higher oversight of any congregation by any individual or group (such as pope, Cardinals, councils, conferences, boards, or anything else). That is a concept of man, not God. We are ruled strictly by God's word, as we study and practice what it contains. The term "deacons" comes from the Greek word diakoneo [dee-ak-on-eh'-o]; to be an attendant as a host, Deacon: minister unto, serve. Their primary duty therefore is to help local congregation as needed.]

In Hebrews 13, the writer mentions "those that rule over you," as also teaching. We can follow their faith as we see their example of dedication to Christ. Directly after this we see "Jesus Christ is the same yesterday, today and forever," indicating that the oversight must be focused on the "pure word of God" without deviation—*because it does not change*. And then comes the warning to not be carried away with various and strange doctrines. *Changed* doctrines, *perversions* of the word of God, were being spread in the first century:

> *I marvel that you are turning away so soon from Him who called you in the grace of Christ, to a different gospel, which is not another; but there are*

some who trouble you and want to per-
vert the gospel of Christ. But even if
we, or an angel from heaven, preach
any other gospel to you then what we
have preached to you, let him be ac-
cursed. As we have said before, so now
I say again, if anyone preaches any
other gospel to you then what you have
received, let him be accursed. For do I
now persuade men, or God? Or do I
seek to please men? For if I still please
men, I would not be a bondservant of
Christ. (Galatians 1:6-10)

Paul is shocked, amazed that they have
turned away to a *different* gospel—not another equally-valid gospel, but a *perverted*
gospel. Something had been added or taken
away from the original teaching. Paul emphasizes twice, "*if anyone does this, let him be*
accursed." Paul ends with a question, "*For*
do I now persuade men, or God?" To persuade men he taught God's word, "the gospel
of Christ." If you change the gospel to something else, what you are really trying to do is
tell God He's wrong—that you can do it better! Pleasing men and tickling their itching

ears is not the job of a preacher. God gave His word to us, we are not giving it to Him! To change the gospel of Christ, God's word, is wrong! If you would like more information on this subject, you can read 1st, 2nd and 3rd John, and the book of Jude. These show the apostles fighting against false teachings coming into the church even in their day.

By Every Word

Section 5:

God's Word vs. the Teachings of Man.

Although we discussed this topic before, I believe we need to look a little closer at the reality that many different doctrines of man don't just disagree with God's word, but also with each other. The opinions of friends, family, and associates all have an impact how we view different subjects. Not every one of them can be right! We have already noted how "truth" is paramount. We must study God's word if we are truly going to understand what God desires for us.

Jesus contended with the same problem in His day, but He knew the truth. Notice how Jesus addresses the Pharisees in Matthew 23:13-15:

> *"Woe to you, teachers of the law and Pharisees, you hypocrites! You shut the door of the kingdom of heaven in people's faces. You yourselves do not enter, nor will you let those enter who are trying to." (NIV)*

Jesus is saying the teachings of the scribes and Pharisees had polluted God's word to the extent that neither they as teachers, nor those listening to them, will be able to enter the kingdom of heaven. If we desire to enter the kingdom of heaven and be saved, we need to listen to the warning. And we need to be incredibly careful who we listen to, constantly comparing what we hear to God's word.

Several things are paramount in properly handling the Scriptures. First, remember 1 John 4:1:

> *Beloved, do not believe every spirit, but test the spirits, whether they are of God; because many false prophets have gone out into the world.*

We have a stern warning here: many false prophets have gone out into the world; so we need to know who they are! Then, Scripture tells us to test the spirits, whether they are of God. This includes everyone! We cannot make any exceptions! Those who are closest to us, such as friends and family, can have a great influence on us. This may be hard to hear, but what they say and do must be scrutinized and compared to the Scriptures. Do you truly understand the consequences of blindly following a false teacher? Jesus said:

> *Every plant that my heavenly Father has not planted will be pulled up by the roots. Leave them; they are blind guides. If the blind lead the blind, both will fall into a pit. (Matthew 15:13-14, NIV)*

After explaining how scribes and Pharisees put commandments and traditions of men before God's commandments, Jesus said:

> *Thus you nullify the word of God for the sake of your tradition. You hypocrites! Isaiah was right when he prophesied about you: "These people honor me with their lips, but their hearts are far from me. They worship me in vain; their teachings are merely human rules." (Matthew 15:7-9, NIV)*

So, when Jesus said, *"Every plant that my heavenly father has not planted will be pulled up by the roots"* (Matthew 15:13, NIV), He makes it plain: these people will not be allowed into the kingdom of heaven! And if they will not be allowed into the kingdom of heaven, how can those following them be allowed in? The followers aren't following God's commandment to "try every spirit" and "study to show yourself approved." It is imperative we make sure no false belief system becomes part of our lives. It is a matter of life and death to us! This is why the next part is critical!

We need to know what is correct and what is false! Again, 2 Timothy 2:15 states, "*Study to show thyself approved unto God, a workman that needs not to be ashamed, rightly dividing the word of truth*" (KJV). I have heard people say they need to leave the interpreting of the Scriptures to the teachers of their group. It's as though the "common believer" is incapable of understanding Scripture accurately. Think about this, would God have given us that command if we were not able to follow it? The truth is, God made every person capable of studying the Scriptures and coming to the knowledge of truth. The Scriptures are written in a simple language for anyone to read and understand. Further, we (all of us) are commanded to try the very spirits of these people who would tell us such a thing.

Matthew 7:7-10 states:

> *Ask and it will be given to you; seek and you will find; knock and the door will be open to you. For everyone who asks receives; the one who seeks finds; and to the one who knocks, the door will be opened. (NIV)*

God makes it clear He gave us the ability to study the Scriptures and understand. If we do so with an open heart, desiring God to do the instructing, we can learn. Everyone needs to approach the Scriptures with, "God, teach me your will," in their hearts. James 1:5, states, "*If any of you lacks wisdom, you should ask God, who gives generously to all without finding fault, and it will be given to you*" (NIV). That is a promise from God! Begin by testing me, and the words that are written here. Compare what I am saying in this writing to God's word and learn *His* will. This is how you can know the truth. Try every spirit, and study to show yourself approved unto God, a workman that needs not to be ashamed rightly dividing the word of truth.

If you go to Matthew 23:23-36, and continue to read this section you will learn other things about the scribes and Pharisees. They were not doing or teaching what they were supposed to. They would pay their tithe of mint and anise, but were ignoring the more important matters such as justice, mercy, and faith. Jesus called them blind guides, they strained on a gnat but could swallow a camel. In other words, they would argue back and forth about some small matter, while some things of real importance would be ignored or shrugged off. Jesus further accused them of being full of extortion and self-indulgence, likening them to whitewashed tombs which are beautiful on the outside but full of dead men's bones—in other words, they were *hypocrites*. Look around you, are many of the so-called teachers of God's word any different from those in Jesus' time?

Let us make another point by looking at Matthew 15:1-9:

*Then the scribes and Pharisees who were from Jerusalem came to Jesus, saying, "Why do Your disciples transgress the tradition of the elders? For they do not wash their hands when they eat bread." He answered and said to them, "**Why do you also transgress the commandment of God because of your tradition?** For God commanded, saying, 'Honor your father and your mother'; and 'He who curses father or mother, let him be put to death.' But you say, 'Whoever says to his father or mother, "Whatever profit you might have received from me is a gift to God"— then he need not honor his father or mother.' **Thus you have made the commandment of God of no effect by your tradition.** Hypocrites! Well did Isaiah prophesy about you, saying: 'These people draw near to Me with their mouth, and honor Me with their lips, but their heart is far from Me. And **in vain they worship Me**, **teaching as doctrines the commandments of men.**'"*

Are the false teachers of today any better? NO, they are not! And did you notice that the traditions and commandments of men had made God's word of no effect? There was no saving value to it! You see, by adding to or subtracting from the word of God, false teachers regularly leave out life-saving information and or cause it to say something totally different. It is changed and is no longer the true saving gospel. This same thought is again echoed in Mark 7:13, *"thus you nullify the word of God by your traditions that you have handed down. And you do many things like that"* (NIV).

Adding and subtracting from Scripture clearly nullifies the promise! Think about that for a second, and answer this question: By obeying false commands, who are you serving, God or man? The answer is simple: You would be obeying man and ignoring God. Therefore, it is important to try every spirit and study the Scriptures yourself to verify what is true versus what is not.

Section 6:

The Word of God vs. the Teacher.

Now let us cover a specific point about teachers who love the praise of men.

> *Then Jesus spoke to the multitudes and to His disciples, saying: "The scribes and the Pharisees sit in Moses' seat. Therefore, whatever they tell you to observe, that observe and do, but do not do according to their works; for they say, and do not do. For they bind heavy burdens, hard to bear, and lay them on men's shoulders; but they themselves will not move them with one of their fingers. But all their works they do to be seen by men. They make their phylacteries broad and enlarge the borders of their garments. They love the best seats at feast, the best seats in the synagogue, greetings in the marketplaces, and to be called by men, 'Rabbi, Rabbi.' But you, do not be called, 'Rabbi'; for one is your teacher, the Christ and you are all brethren. Do not call anyone on earth*

your father; for One is your Father, He who is in heaven. And do not be called teachers; for One is your Teacher, the Christ. But he who is greatest among you shall be your servant. And whoever exalts himself will be humbled, and he who humbles himself will be exalted." (Matthew 23:1-12)

Does any of that sound familiar to you? Do you ever notice people who love to have fancy garments to signify their so-called godliness? How are they different from the scribes and Pharisees that made their phylacteries broad and enlarged the borders of their garments? Don't the same people love the best seats of honor wherever they go? Further did you notice the words "*call no man father, one is your Father*," the one in heaven, our Creator, our God. These men steal His name and status to raise themselves up before you. This is a prime example of desiring the praise of men. We are not even to call someone teacher or Rabbi, because one is your teacher, our Lord and Savior Jesus Christ. Has anyone ever read in the Scriptures where the apostles did such things? Many times, they even worked to support themselves—showing they weren't interested in exalting themselves over their brethren. Also remember whoever exalts himself will be humbled, and the one who humbles himself will be exalted.

I believe it is for this reason that James 3:1 states, *"Not many of you should become teachers, my brothers, for you know that we who teach will be judged with greater strictness"* (ESV). Those of us who teach have a greater responsibility to get the word of God correct because of our influence on those who hear us speak. Therefore we bear a greater responsibility to our Lord and Savior Jesus Christ to make sure that we get this right.

Also look at an important warning in Matthew 7:15-20:

> *Watch out for false prophets. They come to you in sheep's clothing, but inwardly they are ferocious wolves. By their fruit you will recognize them. Do people pick grapes from thornbushes, or figs from thistles? Likewise, every good tree bears good fruit, but a bad*

tree bears bad fruit. A good tree cannot bear bad fruit, and a bad tree cannot bear good fruit. Every tree that does not bear good fruit is cut down and thrown into the fire. Thus, by their fruit you will recognize them (NIV).

How do you know them? By comparing what they teach to the Scriptures. If what they say is true, they can give the book, chapter, and verse for you to verify it. If they cannot show you what they teach in the Scriptures (book, chapter, and verse), or they take the Scriptures out of context (using the Scriptures that ignores the framework of the surrounding verses and related Scriptures), you know they are false teachers.

The apostle Paul dealt with this problem:

I know that after I leave, savage wolves will come in among you and will not spare the flock. Even from your own members men will rise and distort the truth in order to draw away disciples after them. So be on your guard! Remember that for three years I never stop warning each of you night and day with tears. (Acts 20:29-31, NIV)

He warned those he taught, continuously and with tears, not to be drawn away by such men. Can it be any clearer?

By Every Word

Section 7:

God's Word vs. True and False Discipleship.

I have heard it said many times, "I'm a good person; I treat people well and have many friends; I haven't committed any crimes such as stealing and the like; surely I will go to heaven." They might reference Scriptures like Galatians 5:22-25:

> *But the fruit of the Spirit is love, joy, peace, long-suffering, gentleness, goodness, faith, meekness, temperance: against such there is no law. And they that are Christ's have crucified the flesh with the affections and lusts. If we live in the Spirit, let us also walk in the Spirit (KJV)*

They may say, "That's talking about me." They may even brag that they attend church. But consider other parts of Scripture that give a fuller picture:

> *Not everyone who says to me, "Lord, Lord," will enter the kingdom of*

heaven, but only the one who does the will of my Father who is in heaven. Many will say to me on that day, "Lord, Lord, did we not prophesy in your name and in your name drive out demons and in your name perform many miracles?" Then I will tell them plainly, "I never knew you. Away from me, you evildoers!" (Matthew 7:21-23, NIV)

There is clearly something that interferes with their ability to enter into heaven, but what? Also note, these rejected people don't just consider themselves "good, moral people," but they think are working for Christ. The question is, are they in compliance with the Scriptures?

Look at what Jesus said in **John 15:1-9:**

I am the true vine, and My Father is the vinedresser. Every branch in Me that does not bear fruit, He takes away; and every branch that bears fruit, He prunes it so that it may bear more fruit. You are already clean because of the word which I have spoken to you. Remain in Me, and I in you. Just as the branch cannot bear fruit of itself but must remain in the vine, so neither can you unless you remain in Me. I am the vine, you are the branches; the one who remains in Me, and I in him bears much fruit, for apart from Me you can do nothing. If anyone does not remain in Me, he is thrown away like a branch and dries up; and they gather them and throw them into the fire, and they are burned. If you remain in Me, and My words remain in you, ask whatever you wish, and it will be done for you. My Father is glorified by this, that you bear much fruit, and so prove to be My disciples. Just as the Father has loved Me, I also have loved you; remain in My love. (NASB)

There are three main points to be made here.

1. Faithful Christians remember the word "If." It is said of those who are in Christ: "*If you remain in Me, and My words remain in you, ask whatever you wish, and it will be*

done for you. My Father is glorified by this, that you bear much fruit, and so prove to be My disciples. Just as the Father has loved Me, I also have loved you; remain in My love." (NASB) Likewise, John 8:31-32, *"If you abide in my word you are my disciples indeed. And you shall know the truth, and the truth shall make you free."* (NKJV) did you see the word "if"? It's a word that brings with it the idea of a "condition" or "stipulation." That "stipulation" or "condition" is you must remain in Christ by following His words. This group abides in "scriptural truth" as well as "in Christ."

2. Christians who don't remain faithful need to remember the "fire." The ones who do not bear fruit for the Lord, that is, aren't faithful to Him, are told: *"apart from Me you can do nothing. If anyone does not remain in Me, he is thrown away like a branch and dries up; and they gather them and throw them into the fire, and they are burned."* Their condition is no better (and some verses suggest is actually worse) than those who never obeyed the gospel at all.

3. Those who imagine themselves "in Christ," but who are not, need to remember Christ's words, "I never knew you." This is a category many do not think about. Many have not truly obeyed the gospel—they believed the wrong people (i.e., the wrong teaching) and believe they are in Christ when they are not. This of course is an incredibly sad condition.

Let me explain by first going to John 3:1-5.

> *Now there was a man of the Pharisees named Nicodemus, a ruler of the Jews. This man came to Jesus by night and said to him, "Rabbi, we know that you are a teacher come from God, for no one can do these signs that you do unless God is with him." Jesus answered him, "Truly, truly, I say to you, unless one is born again, he cannot see the kingdom of God." Nicodemus said to him, "How can a man be born when he is old? Can he enter a second time into his mother's womb and be born?" Jesus answered, "Truly, truly, I say to*

you, unless one is born of water and the Spirit, he cannot enter the kingdom of God." (ESV)

The key to this saying of Jesus is the water, referring to baptism where you receive the gift of the Holy Spirit. This is clarified in passages like Acts 2:38-39:

Then Peter said to them, "Repent, and each of you be baptized in the name of Jesus Christ for the forgiveness of your sins; and you will receive the gift of the Holy Spirit. For the promise is for you and your children and for all who are far away, as many as the Lord our God will call to Himself." (NASB)

Those who obeyed were born of water and the Spirit, (i.e., born again as some people say.). Notice, their belief in what they were told, caused them to first repent of their sins, a turning away from sinful action as a commitment to never do them again. It was followed by their submission to baptism, as per the divine command.[3]

Baptism is a burial; literally the word means "to immerse or submerge." Colossians 2:12:

> *...having been buried with Him in baptism, **in which** you were also raised up with Him **through faith** in the working of God, who raised Him from the dead. (NASB)*

Can you bury anything by sprinkling or pouring on it? NO! They do not fit the definition! Therefore, the one true Baptism can only be performed by immersing a person in water. In fact, there is no dispute that this was the primary practice of baptism for hundreds of years after Christ until men, using human wisdom, brought in pouring and sprinkling.

---

[3] Note: the word Baptism primarily comes from the word *baptizo*, a derivative of *bapto, to dip, immerse, submerge for a religious purpose*. The word for pouring (rhantizo) and the word for sprinkling (ekcheo) are never translated as baptism as they have a different meaning.

Many people who believe they are Christians have not been taught about baptism correctly.

> *There is one body and one Spirit, just as also you were called in one hope of your calling; one Lord, one faith, <u>one baptism</u>, one God and Father of all who is above all and through all and in all. (Ephesians 4:4-6)*

Clearly, there is only one scriptural baptism: "immersion." And What does it do? Let's let the Bible tell us:

> *Corresponding to that, <u>baptism now saves you</u>, not the removal of dirt from the flesh, but an appeal to God for a good conscience through the resurrection of Jesus Christ. (1 Peter 3:21, NASB)*

The only way one can have a good conscience is to be baptized, because "baptism now saves you." In other words, "baptism removes sins!"

> *No, I tell you, but unless you repent, you will all likewise perish. Or do you think that those eighteen on whom the*

tower in Siloam fell and killed them were worse offenders than all the other people who live in Jerusalem? No, I tell you, but unless you repent, you will all likewise perish. (Luke 13:3-5, NASB)

In Acts 2:38-39, repentance was given as a prerequisite for someone to be baptized on the day of Pentecost. It is also a prerequisite for us today.

Two Very Important Questions,

1. Are you abiding in the vine of our Lord Jesus and bringing forth good fruit?
2. Or are you like the branch that is to be cast into the fire because are not bearing fruit—and if you are not legitimately in Christ, you *cannot* bear Christ's fruit? Perhaps it is due to a misunderstanding of the scriptures, leaving you outside of Christ's body, having not been properly baptized into Christ. The call that Peter made in Acts 2:38-39 applies to you: *"Repent and be baptized every one of you in the name of Jesus Christ for the forgiveness of*

your sins, and you will receive the gift of the Holy Spirit. For the promise is for you and for your children and for all who are far off, everyone whom the Lord our God calls to himself." (ESV)

Section 8:

Key Points

1. 2 Timothy 3:16; "*All Scripture is given by inspiration of God, and is profitable for doctrine, for reproof, for correction, for instruction in right-eousness, that the man of God may be complete, thoroughly equipped for every good work.*" Basically, you can find guidance for everything you do in life!

2. The Commandments are based on love. Matthew 22:37-40, "*You shall love the Lord your God with all your heart, and with all your soul, and with all your mind. This is the greatest and foremost commandment. The second is like it, you shall love your neighbor as yourself.*" Also, 1 John 4:20. "*If someone says, "I love God," and hates his brother, he is a liar; for the one who does not love his brother whom he has seen, cannot love God whom he has not seen.*" (NASB)

3. The word of God will not change. Luke 21:33 & Matthew 24:35:

"*Heaven and earth will pass away, but My words will by no means pass away*" (NKJV). Malachi 3:6, "*For I am the Lord, I do not change.*"

4. Matthew 4:4, "*It is written, Man shall not live by bread alone, but by every word that proceeds from the mouth of God.*"

5. The words Jesus speaks are from God. John 12:47-48, "*And if anyone hears My words and does not believe, I do not judge him; for I did not come to judge the world but to save the world. He who rejects Me, and does not receive My words, has that which judges him—the word that I have spoken will judge him in the last day.*"

6. There will be dire consequences to anyone who tries to change the word of God. Galatians 1:6-10: "*I marvel that you are turning away so soon from Him who called you in the grace of Christ, to a different gospel, which is not another; but there are some who trouble you and want to pervert the gospel of Christ. But even if we, or an angel from heaven, preach any other*"

gospel to you then what we have preached to you, let him be accursed. As we have said before, so now I say again, if anyone preaches any other gospel to you then what you have received, let him be accursed. For do I now persuade men, or God? Or do I seek to please men? For if I still please men, I would not be a bondservant of Christ."

7. There are many teachers in the world who teach falsehood. Their teachings will lead you to destruction. Matthew 7:15-20: *"Watch out for false prophets. They come to you in sheep's clothing, but inwardly they are ferocious wolves. By their fruit you will recognize them"* (NIV).

8. Therefore, 1 John 4:1: *"Beloved, do not believe every spirit, but test the spirits, whether they are of God; because many false prophets have gone out into the world."* (NKJV)

9. Therefore, 2 Timothy 2:15, *"Be diligent to present yourself approve to God, a worker who does not need to*

be ashamed, rightly dividing the word of truth."

10. It is a matter of spiritual life and death to get it right! Matthew 7:21-23: *"Not everyone who says to me, 'Lord, Lord,' will enter the kingdom of heaven, but only the one who does the will of my Father who is in heaven. Many will say to me on that day, 'Lord, Lord, did we not prophesy in your name and in your name drive out demons and in your name perform many miracles?' Then I will tell them plainly, 'I never knew you. Away from me, you evildoers!'"* (NIV)

11. There is a need to be baptized for the remission of sins! Jesus stated in John 3:5:*"Truly, truly, I say to you, unless one is born of water and the Spirit, he cannot enter the kingdom of God."* (ESV) Have you been scripturally baptized for the remission of your sins? If not hear the call of Acts 2:38-39: *"Repent and be baptized every one of you in the name of Jesus Christ for the forgiveness of your sins, and you will receive the gift of the Holy Spirit.*

For the promise is for you and for your children and for all who are far off, everyone whom the Lord our God calls to himself." (ESV) And along with that, 1 Peter 3: 21: "*Corresponding to that, baptism now saves you, not the removal of dirt from the flesh, but an appeal to God for a good conscience through the resurrection of Jesus Christ.*" (NASB)

12. Repentance is also important! Luke 13:3-5: "*No, I tell you, but unless you repent, you will all likewise perish. Or do you think that those eighteen on whom the tower in Siloam fell and killed them were worse offenders than all the other people who live in Jerusalem? No, I tell you, but unless you repent, you will all likewise perish.*" (NASB) (emphasized twice for importance)

I hope the things in this booklet will help you understand the extreme importance of understanding God's word correctly. The apostles spent much time trying to bring people back to what was once delivered. I will close with what is written in 1 John 1:1-4:

> *That which was from the beginning, which we have heard, which we have seen with our eyes, which we have looked upon, and our hands have handled, concerning the Word of life – the life was manifested, and we have seen, and bear witness, and declare to you that eternal life which was from the Father and was manifested to us – that which we have seen and heard we declare to you, that you also may have fellowship with us; and truly our fellowship is with the Father and with His Son Jesus Christ. And these things we write to you that your joy may be full. (NKJV)*

Version and Source Information

King James Version (KJV) Quotations designated (KJV) are Scripture taken from the King James Version – In 1604, King James I of England authorized that a new translation of the Bible into English be started. It was finished in 1611, just 85 years after the first translation of the New Testament into English appeared (Tyndale, 1526). The Authorized Version, or King James Version, quickly became the standard for English-speaking Protestants. Its flowing language and prose rhythm has had a profound influence on the literature of the past 400 years. The King James Version is public domain in the United States.

New King James Version (NKJV) Quotations designated (NKJV) are Scripture taken from the New King James Version®. Copyright © 1982 by Thomas Nelson. Used by permission. All rights reserved.

English Standard Version (ESV) Quotations designated (ESV) are from The Holy Bible, English Standard Version. ESV® Text

Books by Wyeth and Bramble

Baptism: The Often Misunderstood Commandment

Book: $7.99
Workbook: $6.99
Teacher's Manual: $6.99

By Every Word
A study on the authority of Scripture

Book: $7.99
Workbook: $6.99
Teacher's Manual: $6.99

Making Enemies and Brothers
A Study of Paul's Missionary Journeys

Workbook: $12.99
Teacher's Manual: $12.99

Bulk Discounts Available

ChuckWyeth@hotmail.com | (505) 397-4195